The Family Kitchen

VALUE FAMILY MEALS

Contents

hinkler

Published by Hinkler Books Pty Ltd
45–55 Fairchild Street
Heatherton Victoria 3202 Australia
www.hinkler.com.au

Design and layout © Hinkler Books Pty Ltd 2013
Food photography and recipe development
© StockFood, the Food Media Agency
Typesetting: MPS Limited
Prepress: Splitting Image

Image © Shutterstock: Blue bowls © Carlos Yudica

ISBN: 978 1 7430 8329 1

Printed and bound in China

Introduction

Many of the world's greatest cuisines are filled with dishes that are hearty, healthy and made with local, seasonal ingredients – in essence, value meals! Inexpensive staples such as rice, pasta and beans can form the basis of a mouth-watering feast. Rich stews, curries and goulashes make the most of tougher cuts of meat. Low-cost food does not have to compromise flavour, quality or nutrition. In fact, you will probably find that sticking to a budget brings new foods and surprising tastes into your kitchen.

Reduce your costs

All the recipes in this book are for inexpensive, simple and filling meals. The following ideas can reduce recipe costs even further.

- Choose fruits and vegetables that are in season. They are usually cheaper, and their flavours are at their best.

- Replace or supplement animal protein with legumes. For example, use half the quantity of lamb in a bolognese and add some red lentils.

- Less popular cuts of pork, beef and lamb cost less. Cuts such as shanks and shoulders benefit from long, slow cooking, so they are perfect in stews, casseroles and curries.

- Frozen seafood is usually less expensive than fresh, and most frozen vegetables and fruits are cheaper too.

- Less popular fish species – such as basa (river cobbler/bocourti) and Pacific whiting (hake) – cost less, and farmed fish is often less expensive than wild.

- Buy ingredients in bulk to save money in the long term. A well-stocked pantry and freezer will also keep you away from fast-food menus and impulse buys!

- Where possible, plan meals ahead and don't throw away food. Use what you already have in the house – for example, at the end of the week, use up leftover vegetables in a delicious soup or frittata.

Main Meals

Cooking healthy, appetising family meals on a budget is easy with these recipes. You don't need expensive cuts of meat to eat well. Simply add beans and eggs for extra protein, carbohydrate-rich foods such as potatoes and rice to keep everyone feeling full, and lots of fresh vegetables for colour, flavour and nutrition.

Pot au Feu

Serves 4 · Preparation and cooking 1 hour 20 minutes

1 chicken, cut into 8 pieces

salt and pepper

4 tablespoons olive oil

1 tablespoon chopped thyme

2 bay leaves

1 clove garlic, finely diced

200ml (7fl oz/⅞ cup) chicken stock (broth)

8 spring (green) onions, chopped

250g (9oz/2 cups) green asparagus, trimmed and cut into smaller pieces

200g (7oz) small carrots

400g (14oz) small potatoes, scrubbed

1 Heat the oven to 160°C (140°C fan/ 320°F/gas 3).

2 Season the chicken pieces well.

3 Heat the oil in a large frying pan (skillet) and brown the chicken pieces on all sides.

4 Add the thyme, bay leaves and garlic, stir briefly with the chicken, then add the stock (broth).

5 Bring to a boil, add the vegetables and transfer to a casserole dish. Season to taste with salt and pepper.

6 Cook for about 1 hour until the chicken is cooked and the vegetables are tender.

Chilli Con Carne

Serves 4 · Preparation and cooking 1 hour 20 minutes

2 tablespoons oil

1 onion, chopped

1 large tomato, chopped

450g (16oz) lean minced (ground) beef

1 teaspoon chilli powder

1 teaspoon dried oregano

1 small red chilli, seeds removed and finely chopped

450g (16oz) canned red kidney beans in chilli sauce

400g (14oz) canned chopped tomatoes

30g (1oz) dark (semi-sweet) chocolate, 85% cocoa solids

salt to taste

To serve

boiled rice

To garnish

coriander (cilantro)

red capsicum (bell pepper) strips

1 Heat the oil in a large heavy-based pan and add the onions and tomatoes. Cook over a medium heat until soft, then increase the heat and add the minced (ground) beef, stirring for a few minutes until browned. Reduce the heat and add the chilli powder and oregano.

2 Add the chopped chilli to the pan with the kidney beans and tomatoes. Stir well.

3 Stir in the chocolate. Season well with salt, cover the pan and cook gently for 45–60 minutes, until thick, stirring from time to time to avoid the mixture sticking to the bottom of the pan.

4 Serve with boiled rice and garnish with coriander (cilantro) and capsicum (red pepper).

Beef and Vegetable Pie

Makes 1 pie · Preparation and cooking 1 hour

2 tablespoons oil

500g (18oz) lean minced (ground) beef

2 onions, chopped

2 large carrots, diced

1 stick celery, diced

1½ tablespoons plain (all-purpose) flour

1 tablespoon tomato paste (puree)

250ml (9fl oz/1 cup) beef stock (broth)

1 teaspoon Worcestershire sauce

400g (14oz) puff pastry

1 egg yolk, beaten

To garnish

flat-leaf parsley

1   Heat the oil in a large pan and fry the beef until browned. Add the vegetables and cook for 5 minutes.

2   Stir in the flour and cook for 1 minute. Stir in the tomato paste (puree), stock (broth) and Worcestershire sauce. Bring to a boil, reduce the heat, cover and simmer for 20 minutes. Set aside to cool.

3   Heat the oven to 200ºC (180ºC fan/ 400ºF/gas 6). Grease a 25cm (10in) pie or baking dish.

4   Roll out the pastry on a floured work surface. Use $^2/_3$ of the pastry to line the dish.

5   Fill with the meat filling and use the remaining pastry to make a lid. Use the trimmings to make decorations if you wish. Cut slits in the top to allow the steam to escape during baking.

6   Brush the pastry with beaten egg yolk and bake for 20–25 minutes until the pastry is golden and the filling is piping hot. Garnish with parsley.

Potato Tortilla

Serves 4 · Preparation and cooking 45 minutes

2 tablespoons olive oil

500g (18oz) baking potatoes, diced

1 onion, chopped

salt

freshly ground black pepper

4 eggs

4 tablespoons sour cream

1 tablespoon chopped parsley

200g (7oz) canned red kidney beans, drained and rinsed

100g (3½oz) canned corn kernels (sweetcorn), drained

100g (3½oz) turkey roll (turkey ham), cut into strips

To garnish

lettuce

1 Heat the olive oil in a large frying pan (skillet) and fry the potatoes for 10 minutes.

2 Add the onion and fry gently for a further 5 minutes, stirring occasionally, until the potatoes soften. Season with salt and ground black pepper.

3 Whisk together the eggs, sour cream and parsley and stir in the corn kernels (sweetcorn) and beans. Season with salt and ground black pepper.

4 Pour the egg mixture over the potatoes and lay the turkey roll (turkey ham) strips on top. Cook for 10–15 minutes until firm.

5 Heat the grill (broiler).

6 Brown the top under the grill. Cut into 4 pieces and serve garnished with lettuce.

Chickpea, Chicken and Curry Bake

Serves 4 · Preparation and cooking 1 hour 20 minutes

2 tablespoons plain (all-purpose) flour

salt and pepper

8 boneless skinless chicken thighs, cut into chunks

3 tablespoons oil

300g (11oz) canned chickpeas (garbanzo beans), drained

1 onion, finely chopped

1 clove garlic, crushed

2–3 teaspoons curry powder (jerk seasoning)

800g (28oz) canned chopped tomatoes

125ml (4 1/2 fl oz / 1/2 cup) chicken stock (broth)

1/2 teaspoon white (granulated) sugar

100g (3 1/2 oz) feta cheese

1 Heat the oven to 180ºC (160ºC fan/ 350ºF/gas 4).

2 Mix the flour with a seasoning of salt and pepper and toss the chicken pieces until coated.

3 Heat 2 tablespoons oil in a large frying pan (skillet) and quickly brown the chicken on both sides. Put the chicken into a baking dish and add the drained chickpeas (garbanzo beans).

4 Heat the remaining oil in the pan and cook the onion and garlic for about 4 minutes, until softened but not browned. Stir in the curry powder (jerk seasoning) and cook for 1 minute.

5 Add the tomatoes, stock (broth), sugar, salt and pepper to taste and bring to a boil. Reduce the heat and simmer for about 10 minutes, until the mixture thickens, stirring occasionally.

6 Pour the tomato mixture over the chicken pieces to cover completely. Cover the dish and cook in the oven for 30 minutes.

7 Remove from the oven and crumble the feta cheese on top. Cook, uncovered, for a further 10 minutes, until the cheese has melted and the chicken is cooked through.

Pumpkin Bake

Serves 4 · Preparation and cooking 1 hour 10 minutes

4 x 200g (7oz) pumpkin wedges, with skin

2 tablespoons oil, more if needed

salt

1 tablespoon butter

2 cloves garlic, chopped

2 onions, chopped

12 sage leaves

1 tablespoon plain (all-purpose) flour

400ml (14fl oz/1²/₃ cups) milk

200g (7oz) mozarella cheese

1 teaspoon mustard

2 egg yolks

3 tablespoons grated parmesan cheese

1   Heat the oven to 200ºC (180ºC fan/ 400ºF/gas 6).

2   Put the pumpkin wedges in a roasting tin. Drizzle the wedges with 1 tablespoon oil and sprinkle with salt. Bake for about 30 minutes until tender. Set aside to cool.

3   Reduce the oven temperature to 190ºC (170ºC fan/375ºF/gas 5).

4   Peel off the skin from the cooked pumpkin flesh. Cut the pumpkin into thick slices and put into a baking dish.

5   Heat the butter and remaining oil in a frying pan (skillet) and cook the garlic and onions until softened.

6   Add half the sage leaves and tip into a bowl. Set aside.

7   Sprinkle the flour into the pan, adding more butter or oil if the mixture looks too dry, and mix to a paste. Cook for 1 minute, stirring constantly.

8   Gradually pour in the milk and bring the sauce to a simmer, stirring constantly. Add half the mozarella cheese and the mustard and remove the pan from the heat.

9   Stir in the onion mixture and whisk in the egg yolks. Pour the sauce all over the pumpkin and scatter with the remaining mozarella cheese, sage leaves and the parmesan cheese. Bake for about 15–20 minutes, until bubbling and the cheese has melted.

Fish and Vegetable Bake

Serves 4 · Preparation and cooking 30 minutes

4 x 170g (6oz) firm white fish steaks, e.g. coley (pollock), cod, Pacific whiting (hake)

2 zucchini (courgettes), sliced

2 tablespoons olive oil

200g (7oz) cherry tomatoes

125g (4½oz) green (string) beans, topped and tailed

salt

freshly ground black pepper

To garnish

2 tablespoons chopped flat-leaf parsley

1 Heat the oven to 200ºC (180ºC fan/ 400ºF/gas 6).

2 Put the fish and zucchini (courgettes) into a large baking dish and drizzle with half the oil. Cook for 5 minutes.

3 Add the cherry tomatoes and green (string) beans to the dish. Season to taste with salt and black pepper and drizzle with the remaining oil.

4 Cook for a further 15 minutes, until the fish is cooked and the vegetables are tender.

5 Sprinkle with the parsley and serve immediately.

Fish Cakes

Makes 4 · Preparation and cooking 45 minutes + 30 minutes chilling

450g (16oz) white fish fillets, e.g. coley (pollock), cod, Pacific whiting (hake)

2 bay leaves (optional)

150ml (5fl oz/^{2}/$_3$ cup) milk

150ml (5fl oz/^{2}/$_3$ cup) water

350g (12oz) potatoes, cut into chunks

salt and pepper

30g (1oz/^{1}/$_4$ cup) butter

1 tablespoon chopped flat-leaf parsley

1 tablespoon snipped chives

flour, for dusting

1 egg, beaten

85g (3oz/1^1/$_2$ cups) slightly stale breadcrumbs

3–4 tablespoons oil, for frying

1 Put the fish and bay leaves in a frying pan (skillet). Pour over the milk and water. Cover, bring to a boil, then reduce the heat and simmer for 4 minutes. Remove from the heat and leave to stand, covered, for 10 minutes.

2 Put the potatoes into a pan and just cover with water. Add a pinch of salt, bring to a boil, then simmer for 10–15 minutes, until tender.

3 Lift the fish out of the milk with a slotted spoon and place on a plate to cool.

4 Drain the potatoes then mash with the butter. Season well with salt and pepper. Stir in the parsley and chives.

5 Flake the fish into the pan of potatoes. Mix together gently with your hands.

6 On a lightly floured surface, carefully shape the mixture into 4 cakes, about 2.5cm (1in) thick.

7 Dip each cake into the beaten egg, brushing over the top and sides until completely coated.

8 Coat the cakes in the crumbs, patting the crumbs on the sides and tops so they are lightly covered. Put onto a plate, cover and chill for 30 minutes.

9 Heat the oil in a large frying pan. Fry the fish cakes for about 5 minutes on each side, until crisp and golden. Serve with peas.

Lentil and Vegetable Curry

Serves 4 · Preparation and cooking 1 hour

1 large eggplant (aubergine), cut into chunks

1 green capsicum (bell pepper), seeds removed, sliced

1 yellow capsicum (bell pepper), seeds removed, sliced

1 red capsicum (bell pepper), seeds removed, sliced

4 tablespoons oil

1 teaspoon mild chilli powder

1 onion, chopped

1 teaspoon black mustard seeds

2 tablespoons curry paste

145g (5oz/¾ cup) dried red lentils

1 small cauliflower, cut into florets

500ml (18fl oz/2 cups) vegetable stock (broth)

To garnish

coriander (cilantro) leaves

1 Heat the oven to 190ºC (170ºC fan/ 375ºF/gas 5).

2 Put the eggplant (aubergine) and capsicums (peppers) in a small roasting tin or baking dish. Drizzle with 3 tablespoons oil and sprinkle with the chilli powder. Stir well to coat, then cook for 20–25 minutes, until tender and golden brown.

3 Heat the remaining oil in a pan. Gently cook the onion for 5 minutes, until soft. Add the black mustard seeds and cook until they 'pop', then stir in the curry paste.

4 Stir in the lentils, cauliflower and stock (broth) and bring to a boil. Reduce the heat and simmer for 15–20 minutes, until the lentils and cauliflower are tender.

5 Stir in the capsicums and eggplant. Serve with boiled rice and garnish with coriander (cilantro).

Casseroles and Stews

Casseroles and stews are a fantastic way to cut costs without cutting out flavour. Take a tour of some of the world's finest cuisines with these dishes. Use inexpensive ingredients – such as tougher cuts of meat – and longer cooking times, and enjoy the resulting rich aromas and tastes.

Beef Stew

Serves 4 · Preparation and cooking 3 hours 20 minutes

3 tablespoons oil

900g (32oz) casserole steak (stewing beef), cut into 3cm (1½in) pieces

2 onions, coarsely chopped

1 clove garlic, crushed (optional)

4 carrots, coarsely chopped

1 tablespoon plain (all-purpose) flour

1 teaspoon ground allspice

salt and pepper

100ml (3½fl oz/³/₈ cup) dark beer

500ml (18fl oz/2 cups) beef stock (broth)

2 bay leaves

1 tablespoon black treacle (molasses) or brown sugar

1 Heat the oven to 160ºC (140ºC fan/ 320ºF/gas 3).

2 Heat the oil in a flameproof casserole dish or large pan and add the meat in batches. Fry quickly until brown on all sides. Remove the meat and set aside.

3 Add the chopped onions, garlic and carrots to the fat left in the casserole dish and cook for a few minutes until lightly browned.

4 Add the flour, allspice, salt and pepper and cook for 1 minute, stirring, before adding the beer, beef stock (broth), bay leaves and molasses (treacle) to the pan.

5 Bring to a boil, stirring constantly. Add the meat and cover the dish. If using a pan, put into a deep baking dish.

6 Transfer to the oven and cook for 2–3 hours, until the meat is very tender but not stringy.

Osso Buco

Serves 4 · Preparation and cooking 2 hours 20 minutes

30g (1oz/¼ cup) plain (all-purpose) flour

½ teaspoon salt

¼ teaspoon pepper

4 rose veal shanks

1 tablespoon butter

2 tablespoons oil

1 onion, finely chopped

2 carrots, sliced

1 stick celery, sliced

4 large potatoes, diced

2 cloves garlic, crushed

250ml (9fl oz/1 cup) veal or vegetable stock (broth)

400g (14oz) canned chopped tomatoes

For the gremolata

1 large unwaxed lemon, finely grated zest

½ clove garlic, finely chopped

To garnish

flat-leaf parsley, finely chopped

1 Mix together the flour, salt and pepper and coat the rose veal shanks on all sides.

2 Heat the butter and oil in a frying pan (skillet) and cook the rose veal shanks until browned on all sides. Set aside.

3 Add the onion, carrots, celery, potatoes and garlic to the pan and cook, stirring, for 3–4 minutes. Transfer the vegetables to a large pan. Put the rose veal shanks on top of the vegetables.

4 Pour off the fat from the frying pan and pour in the stock (broth) and tomatoes. Bring to a boil and simmer for 2 minutes, scraping the residue from the base of the pan. Pour over the veal and vegetables.

5 Bring to a boil then reduce the heat, cover and simmer gently for 1–2 hours until the meat is very tender and the sauce is thick. Turn the veal shanks twice during the cooking time. When turning the shanks, lift them gently so that they stay in one piece and the marrow is not lost.

For the gremolata

1 Mix together all the ingredients and place in a small serving bowl.

To serve

1 Serve garnished with parsley and a small bowl of gremolata.

Potato and Bean Goulash with Sausages

Serves 4 · Preparation and cooking 40 minutes

2 tablespoons oil

30g (1oz) butter

1 onion, chopped

1 teaspoon paprika

375g (13oz) spicy German or Hungarian sausage, sliced into chunks

500g (18oz) potatoes, cut into bite-sized chunks

125g (4½oz) canned chopped tomatoes

1 bay leaf

250ml (9fl oz/1 cup) vegetable stock (broth) or water

100g (3½oz) green (string) beans, chopped

salt

freshly ground black pepper

1 Heat the oil and butter in a large heavy-based pan and fry the onion for a few minutes until softened but not browned.

2 Add the paprika and cook for 1 minute, then add the sausage and cook until lightly browned.

3 Add the potatoes, tomatoes, bay leaf and stock (broth). Stir and bring to a boil.

4 Reduce the heat and simmer for 15 minutes, stirring occasionally, until the vegetables are tender.

5 Add the green (string) beans and cook for a further 5 minutes until tender. Season to taste with salt and pepper.

Spicy Pork Ragout

Serves 4 · Preparation and cooking 2 hours

3 tablespoons oil

900g (32oz) pork neck, cut into cubes

1 onion, chopped

1 stick celery, chopped

1 clove garlic, chopped

1 teaspoon paprika

1 teaspoon cumin seeds

1 carrot, chopped

400g (14oz) canned
tomatoes, chopped

1 tablespoon tomato paste (puree)

250ml (9fl oz/1 cup) red wine

250ml (9fl oz/1 cup) meat stock (broth)

oregano leaves

1 Heat the oil in a large pan and brown the meat on all sides. Remove the meat from the pan and set aside.

2 Gently cook the onion and celery until soft but not brown, then add the garlic, paprika and cumin seeds.

3 Cook for 2 minutes then add the carrot, tomatoes and tomato paste (puree). Return the meat to the pan, pour over the wine and let bubble.

4 Add the stock (broth) and parsley, bring to a simmer and cook very gently for 1 1/2 hours or until the meat is very tender. Add a little water during cooking if necessary. Garnish with oregano leaves.

Chicken and Vegetable Casserole

Serves 4 · Preparation and cooking 1 hour 10 minutes

2 tablespoons oil

4 bone-in skin-on chicken joints

15g (1/2oz/1/8 cup) plain (all-purpose) flour

salt and pepper

1 onion, finely chopped

4 rashers bacon, rind removed, chopped

2 cloves garlic, finely chopped

2 large potatoes, diced

2 large carrots, chopped

125g (41/2oz) pearl barley

750ml (26fl oz/3 cups) chicken stock (broth)

2 tablespoons Dijon mustard

To garnish

1 tablespoon chopped flat-leaf parsley

1   Heat the oven to 180°C (160°C fan/ 350°F/gas 4).

2   Heat the oil in a large frying pan (skillet). Toss the chicken in the flour with some seasoning, then brown for 4 minutes until golden. Remove from the pan and set aside.

3   Add the onion, bacon, garlic, potatoes and carrots to the pan, and cook for a few minutes, stirring.

4   Stir in the barley, stock (broth) and mustard, then return the chicken to the pan and stir to combine.

5   Put into a casserole or baking dish and cook for 45–55 minutes, until the chicken and vegetables are tender.

6   Put onto warmed serving plates and garnish with parsley.

Chicken and Lentil Stew

Serves 4 · Preparation and cooking 1 hour 20 minutes

6–8 chicken thighs

2 tablespoons plain (all-purpose) flour

salt and pepper

3 tablespoons oil

2 onions, chopped

1 leek, sliced

4–5 carrots, sliced

1 small swede (rutabaga), chopped

110g (4oz/½ cup) green (Puy) lentils

500ml (18fl oz/2 cups) chicken stock (broth)

1 teaspoon dried mixed herbs

1 Toss the chicken in the flour, salt and pepper until coated.

2 Heat 2 tablespoons oil in a large pan and quickly brown the chicken pieces. Remove from the pan and set aside.

3 Add the remaining oil to the pan and gently cook the onion until starting to soften. Add the remaining vegetables and the lentils and cook for 4 minutes.

4 Add the chicken to the pan and pour in the stock (broth) and herbs. Season to taste with salt and pepper.

5 Cover the pan with a tight fitting lid and simmer for about 1 hour until the chicken and vegetables are tender. If the stew becomes too dry during cooking, add a little hot water.

Moussaka

Serves 4 · Preparation and cooking 1 hour 25 minutes

2 tablespoons olive oil

1 onion, chopped

2 cloves garlic, chopped

2 eggplants (aubergines), sliced

1 red capsicum (bell pepper), seeds removed, cut into strips

1 green capsicum (bell pepper), seeds removed, cut into strips

600g (21oz) minced (ground) lamb

150ml (5fl oz/^{2}/$_3$ cup) dry red or white wine

400g (14oz) canned chopped tomatoes

salt

freshly ground black pepper

1 tablespoon dried oregano

1 Heat the oven to 200ºC (180ºC fan/ 400ºF/gas 6).

2 Heat the oil in a pan and gently cook the onion and garlic until softened but not browned. Remove from the pan and set aside.

3 Add the eggplants (aubergines) and capsicums (peppers) to the pan and cook until lightly browned and starting to soften. Remove from the pan and set aside.

4 Add the lamb to the pan and quickly brown, stirring.

5 Pour in the wine and cook until almost evaporated. Add the tomatoes. Season with salt and pepper. Stir in the oregano and simmer gently for 15–20 minutes.

6 Arrange the eggplants and the capsicums in a round baking dish so they overlap. Add the lamb mixture, onions and garlic.

7 Cook for 35–40 minutes until piping hot and the vegetables are tender. Serve immediately.

Pasta and Rice

Pasta and rice dishes make terrific,
low-cost meals. They are healthy, versatile
and a great way to fill empty stomachs!
With dishes ranging from classic macaroni
and cheese to spicy jambalaya, you are sure
to find the perfect pasta or rice meal
to satisfy your family.

Spaghetti with Meatballs

Serves 4 · Preparation and cooking 1 hour

For the meatballs

2 tablespoons olive oil

1 onion, finely chopped

400g (14oz) minced (ground) beef

1 teaspoon dried mixed herbs

salt and pepper

1 egg, beaten

2 tablespoons oil, for frying

For the sauce

2 tablespoons olive oil

1 onion, finely chopped

1 clove garlic, chopped

400g (14oz) canned
chopped tomatoes

1 teaspoon white (granulated) sugar

1 tablespoon tomato paste (puree)

To serve

400g (14oz) spaghetti

basil leaves

For the meatballs

1 Heat the oil in a wide pan and gently fry the onion for about 5 minutes or until soft. Stir in the meat, turn up the heat and cook for 5 minutes, stirring all the time.

2 Add the mixed herbs, season with salt and pepper, and remove the pan from the heat.

For the sauce

1 Heat the oil in a pan and gently fry the onion and garlic for 5 minutes or until soft. Add the tomatoes and simmer gently for 20 minutes, stirring from time to time.

2 Stir in the sugar and tomato paste (puree) and season with salt and pepper. Remove the pan from the heat.

To serve

1 Put a large pan of salted water to boil and cook the spaghetti according to the packet instructions.

2 Meanwhile, mix the beaten egg into the meat mixture and roll between your hands to form into meatballs. Heat the oil in a large frying pan (skillet) and gently fry the meatballs until browned well and cooked through.

3 Reheat the sauce, gently stir in the meatballs and serve with the spaghetti. Garnish with basil leaves.

Beef Cannelloni

Serves 4–6 · Preparation and cooking 1 hour 50 minutes

500g (18oz) lean minced (ground) beef

1 onion, chopped

2 teaspoons chopped thyme leaves

2 teaspoons chopped oregano leaves

800g (28oz) canned chopped tomatoes

3 tablespoons tomato paste (puree)

salt and pepper

225g (8oz) button (white) mushrooms, chopped

250g (9oz) dried cannelloni shells

275ml (10fl oz/1$\frac{1}{8}$ cups) milk

2 tablespoons cornflour (cornstarch)

110g (4oz/1 cup) grated mozzarella cheese

110g (4oz/1 cup) grated mature cheddar cheese

To garnish

flat-leaf parsley

1 Heat the oven to 180°C (160°C fan/ 350°F/gas 4).

2 Dry-fry the minced (ground) beef in a large frying pan (skillet) for 5 minutes until browned. Add the onion and cook for a further 5 minutes. Stir in the herbs and half the tomatoes with 2 tablespoons tomato paste (puree).

3 Season with salt and pepper and simmer for 15 minutes. Stir in the mushrooms and cook for a further 10 minutes.

4 Heat the remaining tomatoes and paste together for 10 minutes. Spoon a little of the tomato mixture over the base of a 1.7l (3 UK pt/3.5 US pt) baking dish.

5 Fill each cannelloni shell with the mince mixture. Carefully cover the tomato mixture with a layer of filled cannelloni shells. Spoon over some more tomato mixture. Lay the remaining shells over the tomato mixture and then spoon any excess meat mixture over the shells.

6 Heat the milk in a pan to a boil. Mix the cornflour (cornstarch) with enough cold water to form a smooth paste. Stir the cornflour into the milk and simmer for five minutes until thickened. Season with salt and pepper and stir in the mozzarella cheese.

7 Pour the cheese sauce over the cannelloni shells and top with the grated cheddar cheese. Bake for 40 minutes until browned and bubbling. Garnish with flat-leaf parsley.

Penne with Chicken and Pesto

Serves 4 · Preparation and cooking 35 minutes

400g (14oz) dried penne

4 boneless skinless chicken breasts

salt

2 tablespoons olive oil

2 zucchini (courgettes), sliced

110g (4oz) button (white) mushrooms, sliced

1 onion, finely chopped

2 cloves garlic, finely chopped

120ml (4fl oz/½ cup) chicken stock (broth)

225g (8oz) spinach

freshly ground black pepper

60ml (2fl oz/¼ cup) pesto

60ml (2fl oz/¼ cup) cream, 18% fat

1 Bring a large pan of salted water to a boil. Add the pasta and cook until 'al dente'.

2 Season the chicken breasts with salt. Heat the oil in a frying pan (skillet) and quickly brown the chicken breasts on both sides. Remove from the pan and set aside. Quickly cook the zucchini (courgettes) and mushrooms in the pan until lightly browned, then set aside.

3 Add the onion to the pan and cook, stirring for 2–3 minutes. Add the garlic and cook for 1 minute. Add the stock (broth) and bring to a boil. Boil vigorously until the liquid is reduced by half.

4 Cut the chicken into pieces and add to the pan with the spinach. Cook, stirring, for 2–3 minutes, until the spinach is wilted and the chicken is cooked through.

5 Remove the pan from the heat and season to taste with pepper. Stir in the zucchini, mushrooms and pesto, followed by the cream and continue stirring until blended.

6 Drain the pasta and put into a large bowl. Add the contents of the pan to the pasta and mix well. Serve immediately.

Fish Lasagne

Serves 4 · Preparation and cooking 1 hour

9 dried lasagne sheets

4 tablespoons olive oil

2 cloves garlic, finely chopped

2 red onions, finely chopped

400g (14oz) canned chopped tomatoes

100g (3¹/₂oz) tomato paste (puree)

100g (3¹/₂oz) capers, rinsed

800g (28oz) white fish fillets, e.g. coley (pollock), cod, Pacific whiting (hake)

1 tablespoon lemon juice

400g (14oz) cherry tomatoes, halved

1 bunch dill (dill weed), finely chopped

salt and pepper

100g (3¹/₂oz/1 cup) grated cheddar cheese

1 Soak the lasagne in plenty of cold water for 10 minutes.

2 Heat 1 tablespoon oil in a large frying pan (skillet). Gently cook the garlic and onions until softened but not browned.

3 Add the canned tomatoes, tomato paste (puree) and capers and simmer for about 20 minutes until reduced.

4 Heat the oven to 180°C (160°C fan/350°F/gas 4). Grease a baking dish.

5 Sprinkle the fish with lemon juice and cut into long strips about 2.5cm (1in) wide. Heat 3 tablespoons oil in a frying pan and briefly fry the fish. Remove from the pan and set aside.

6 Remove the tomato mixture from the heat and stir in the cherry tomatoes and dill (dill weed). Season with salt and pepper.

7 Place alternate layers of well drained lasagne, tomato mixture and fish in the baking dish, finishing with tomato mixture. Sprinkle with grated cheese and bake for 20–25 minutes until the fish is cooked and the top is golden.

Simple Spaghetti

Serves 4 · Preparation and cooking 25 minutes

400g (14oz) dried spaghetti

4 tablespoons olive oil

2 red chillies, seeds removed, sliced

6 cloves garlic, sliced

1–2 tablespoons chopped mint

salt

freshly ground black pepper

To garnish

mint leaves

1 Bring a large pan of salted water to a boil. Add the pasta and cook until 'al dente'.

2 Heat the oil in a large frying pan (skillet) over a low heat. Add the chillies and cook for 1 minute. Add the garlic and cook, stirring for 2 minutes.

3 Remove from the heat, allow to cool slightly, then stir in the mint.

4 Drain the pasta and put into a large bowl. Add the contents of the pan to the pasta and mix well. Season to taste with salt and pepper. Garnish with mint.

Macaroni and Cheese

Serves 4 · Preparation and cooking 30 minutes

30g (1oz/¹/₈ cup) butter

1 clove garlic, finely sliced

2 tomatoes, sliced

750g (26oz) fresh or cooked macaroni

750ml (26fl oz/3 cups) ready-made cheese sauce

75g (2¹/₂oz/1¹/₂ cups) fresh coarse breadcrumbs

185g (6¹/₂oz/1 cup) grated parmesan cheese

1 Heat the oven to 190ºC (170ºC fan/ 375ºF/gas 5).

2 Rub the butter over the base and sides of an ovenproof dish.

3 Scatter the garlic and tomato slices on the base of the dish and add the macaroni.

4 Pour over the sauce, scatter over the breadcrumbs and parmesan and bake in the oven for 20–25 minutes.

Pesto Chicken Risotto

Serves 4 · Preparation and cooking 45 minutes

400g (14oz) chicken breast fillets, cut into wide strips

salt and pepper

2 tablespoons plain (all-purpose) flour

4 tablespoons olive oil

1 tablespoon butter

2 cloves garlic, finely chopped

1 onion, finely chopped

400g (14oz) risotto rice

200ml (7fl oz/⁷⁄₈ cup) white wine

1l (35fl oz/4 cups) hot chicken stock (broth)

1¹⁄₂ tablespoons pesto

1 tablespoon pine nuts

To garnish

rocket (arugula)

1 Season the chicken strips with salt and pepper and coat in flour. Set aside.

2 Heat half the oil and all the butter in a pan and gently cook the garlic and onion until translucent. Add the rice and stir to coat the rice.

3 Add half the wine and stir over the heat until it has evaporated. Add the remaining wine and stir until it has evaporated again. Add 1 ladleful of stock (broth) and cook until it has been absorbed, stirring frequently. Continue in this way, adding a ladleful of stock until the last one has been absorbed and the rice is cooked (but still retains a little bite). If there is not enough stock, continue adding hot water instead.

4 When the rice is cooked stir in the pesto and pine nuts. Season to taste with salt and pepper. Keep warm.

5 Heat the remaining oil in a frying pan (skillet) and fry the chicken pieces until golden brown on both sides. Combine with the risotto and serve immediately garnished with rocket (arugula).

Vegetable and Bean Risotto

Serves 4 · Preparation and cooking 45 minutes

2 tablespoons olive oil

170g (6oz) carrots, diced

1 red capsicum (bell pepper), seeds removed, chopped

2 cloves garlic, crushed

300g (11oz/1½ cups) risotto rice

1.2l (2 UK pt/2.5 US pt/5 cups) hot vegetable stock (broth)

400g (14oz) canned cannellini (white kidney) beans, drained and rinsed

salt

freshly ground black pepper

To garnish

coriander (cilantro)

1 Heat the oil in a wide shallow pan and cook the carrots, capsicum (pepper) and garlic over a low heat for 10 minutes, until softened but not browned.

2 Add the rice to the vegetables and stir for 1 minute, until the grains are glossy.

3 Add a ladleful of stock (broth) to the rice. Stir continuously until it has been absorbed. Continue adding the stock a ladleful at a time, and stirring, for 25–30 minutes until the rice and vegetables are tender.

4 Add the cannellini (white kidney) beans for the last 5 minutes of cooking.

5 Remove the pan from the heat and season to taste with salt and pepper. Put into warmed serving bowls and garnish with coriander (cilantro).

Jambalaya

Serves 4 · Preparation and cooking 50 minutes

4 boneless skinless chicken breasts

3 tablespoons olive oil

1 red onion, chopped

2 cloves garlic, chopped

3 spring (green) onions, sliced into rings

2 red capsicums (bell peppers), seeds removed, finely sliced

1 stick (rib) celery, chopped

2 red chilli peppers, seeds removed, finely sliced

250g (9oz/1 1/8 cups) long-grain rice

500ml (18fl oz/2 cups) chicken stock (broth)

1 bay leaf

salt and pepper

145g (5oz) canned tomatoes, chopped

2 tablespoons coriander (cilantro) leaves, chopped

ground cumin

1 Rinse the chicken breasts and pat dry. Slice into strips.

2 Heat the oil in a pan and gently cook the onion, garlic and spring (green) onions for 2–3 minutes. Add the chicken and continue to cook for 1–2 minutes more.

3 Stir in the capsicum (bell pepper) strips, celery, chilli and rice. Pour in the chicken stock (broth) and add the bay leaf. Season with salt and pepper.

4 Cover and simmer for about 20 minutes, stirring occasionally. When the rice is cooked, add the tomatoes and coriander (cilantro) leaves.

5 Season to taste with the cumin, salt and pepper.

Sides and Snacks

Ready-made or instant side dishes and packaged snacks can really add to the cost of your grocery bill. Preparing your own sides and snacks means that you can keep costs down, and also keep track of what goes into your food, which is healthier for your family.

Tomato Soup

Serves 4 · Preparation and cooking 1 hour 10 minutes

2 tablespoons olive oil

1 onion, chopped

1 carrot, chopped

1 stick celery, chopped

3 teaspoons tomato paste (puree)

1kg (2.2lb) ripe tomatoes, quartered

2 bay leaves

1 pinch white (granulated) sugar

freshly ground black pepper

1.2l (2 UK pt/2.5 US pt/5 cups) hot vegetable stock (broth)

salt

To garnish

finely chopped thyme

1 Heat the oil in a large pan and gently cook the onion, carrot and celery over a low heat for about 10 minutes, until softened.

2 Add the tomato paste (puree), tomatoes, bay leaves and sugar and mix well. Cover and cook over a low heat for 10 minutes, shaking the pan from time to time.

3 Add the pepper to taste as well as the stock (broth) and bring to a boil. Reduce the heat and simmer for about 25 minutes, until the tomatoes have broken down. Remove from the heat, remove the bay leaves and allow to cool slightly.

4 Ladle the mixture in batches into a blender or food processor and blend until smooth. Pour the soup into a bowl after each batch.

5 Return the soup to the pan and heat until piping hot. Add salt to taste.

6 Serve garnished with thyme.

Welsh Rarebit

Serves 4 · Preparation and cooking 15 minutes

250g (9oz/2¼ cups) grated strong cheese, e.g. cheddar

1 tablespoon butter

3 teaspoons Worcestershire sauce

1 teaspoon mustard powder

2 teaspoons plain (all-purpose) flour

freshly ground pepper

4 tablespoons milk or dark beer

4 slices bread

1 Heat the grill (broiler).

2 Put the cheese, butter, Worcestershire sauce, mustard powder, flour and a grinding of pepper into a pan. Mix well and stir in the milk or beer.

3 Stir over a very low heat until melted to a paste. Remove from the heat and set aside to cool slightly.

4 Toast the bread on one side only.

5 Spread the rarebit over the untoasted side and place under the grill until browned and bubbling.

Baked Potatoes with Tuna

Serves 4 · Preparation and cooking 1 hour 40 minutes

4 large potatoes

oil

4 spring (green) onions, chopped

2 tablespoons snipped chives

400g (14oz) canned tuna, drained

3 tablespoons plain yoghurt

1 tablespoon mayonnaise

freshly ground black pepper, to taste

1 Heat the oven to 200°C (180°C fan/ 400°F/gas 6).

2 Rub the potatoes lightly with oil and place on a baking tray (sheet). Prick several times with a fork and bake for 1–1½ hours until tender.

3 Mix together the remaining ingredients until well combined.

4 Split open the potatoes and divide the filling evenly between them.

Sweet Potato Wedges

Serves 4 · Preparation and cooking 50 minutes

4–6 sweet potatoes (yams),
cut into wedges

4 tablespoons olive oil

salt

freshly ground black pepper

1 Heat the oven to 200ºC (180ºC fan/
400ºF/gas 6).

2 Toss the potato (yam) wedges in the oil and
season generously with salt and pepper.

3 Put into a roasting tin or large baking dish in
a single layer and bake for 30–40 minutes
until tender.

Moroccan Vegetables

**Serves 4 · Preparation and cooking 8 hours slow cooking or
2 hours conventional cooking**

2 tablespoons oil

1 onion, chopped

4 carrots, chopped

1 red capsicum (bell pepper), seeds
removed, chopped

2 cloves garlic, crushed

1 small orange pumpkin, roughly chopped

400g (14oz) canned chopped tomatoes

2 teaspoons chilli paste

1 teaspoon ground turmeric

250ml (9fl oz/1 cup) vegetable
stock (broth)

salt and pepper

200g (7oz) zucchini (courgettes),
thickly sliced

400g (14oz) canned chickpeas (garbanzo
beans), drained

To garnish

mint leaves

1   Preheat the slow cooker if necessary – see
    manufacturer's instructions.

2   Heat the oil in a frying pan (skillet) and cook
    the onion for 5 minutes.

3   Add the carrots, capsicum (bell pepper),
    garlic, pumpkin and tomatoes. Stir and add
    the chilli paste and turmeric.

4   Pour in the stock (broth) and season to
    taste with salt and pepper. Bring to a boil.

5   Transfer the mixture to the slow cooker pot.
    The vegetables should be submerged in
    the liquid.

6   Cover and cook on low for 6–8 hours until
    the vegetables are tender.

7   Stir in the zucchini (courgettes) and
    chickpeas (garbanzo beans) and cook on
    high for 15–20 minutes, until the zucchini
    is tender.

8   Serve garnished with torn mint leaves.

For conventional cooking

Heat the oven to 180ºC (160ºC fan/350ºF/gas 4).
Follow the recipe from step 2 to the end of step 4.
Transfer the mixture to a baking dish. Cover and
cook in the oven for about 25 minutes, until the
vegetables are almost tender. Add the zucchini
and continue cooking for another 15–20 minutes
until the zucchini is tender.

Rice Salad

Serves 4 · Preparation and cooking 20 minutes

250g (9oz/1¹⁄₈ cups) long-grain rice

2 carrots, diced

200g (7oz) green (string) beans, cut into bite-size pieces

2 zucchini (courgettes), chopped

50g (1³⁄₄oz) anchovies in oil, drained and chopped

150g (5oz) firm tofu, diced

¹⁄₂ tablespoon capers, rinsed

1 tablespoon chopped mint

3 tablespoons olive oil

1 lemon, finely grated zest and juice

salt and pepper

1 Cook the rice in a pan of boiling salted water for 6 minutes. Add the carrots, green (string) beans and zucchini (courgettes) and cook for a further 4–5 minutes until the rice is cooked and the vegetables are slightly crunchy.

2 Drain well and put into a bowl. Stir in the remaining ingredients and mix well with a fork. Season to taste with salt and pepper.

3 Put into a serving dish and leave to become cold.

Desserts and Cakes

Sticking to a budget doesn't mean you have to skip dessert! These desserts and cakes use low-cost ingredients and are easy to make. Try simple, traditional favourites such as rice pudding, pancakes and carrot cake. Or for a special occasion, create an impression with Eton mess or a chocolate roulade.

Choc-Chip Bread and Butter Pudding

Serves 4 · Preparation and cooking 1 hour + 30 minutes standing

8 slices bread

55g (2oz/¼ cup) butter

170g (6oz/1 cup) chocolate chips

2 teaspoons ground cinnamon
(optional)

400ml (14fl oz/1²/₃ cups) milk

2 eggs

55g (2oz/¼ cup) white
 (granulated) sugar

1   Lightly butter a 1l (1.75 UK pt/2 US pt) pie or
    baking dish.

2   Spread the butter on 1 side of each slice of
    bread and slice diagonally in half. Place a
    layer of bread, buttered-side up, in the base
    of the dish, then add a layer of chocolate
    chips. Sprinkle with a little cinnamon if
    using, then repeat the layers of bread and
    chocolate chips, sprinkling with cinnamon,
    until all the bread is used. Finish with a layer
    of bread and then set aside.

3   Gently warm the milk in a pan over a low
    heat to scalding point. Do not boil.

4   Beat the eggs with ³/₄ of the sugar and
    whisk until pale and frothy.

5   Add the warm milk and stir well, then pour
    the custard over the bread layers and
    sprinkle with the remaining sugar. Leave to
    stand for 30 minutes.

6   Heat the oven to 180°C (160°C fan/
    350°F/gas 4).

7   Cook for 30–40 minutes, until the custard
    has set and the top is golden brown.

Rice Pudding

Serves 4· Preparation and cooking 2 hours 20 minutes

2 teaspoons of butter for dish plus
1 tablespoon butter, in small pieces

40g (1¹/₂oz / ¹/₆ cup) short-grain pudding
rice or sushi rice

30g (1oz/¹/₈ cup) white (granulated) sugar

600ml (21fl oz/2¹/₂ cups) full-cream milk

freshly grated nutmeg (mace) (optional)

1 Heat the oven to 150ºC (130ºC fan/300ºF/
gas 2). Lightly butter a 900ml (1.5 UK pt/
2 US pt) ovenproof dish.

2 Rinse the rice under cold water, drain
well and place in the dish with the sugar
and butter pieces.

3 Pour in the milk and stir well. Sprinkle with a
generous grating of nutmeg (mace), if using.

4 Cook for 1¹/₂–2 hours, stirring after the
first 30 minutes, until golden brown on
top and with a soft, creamy texture. If the
pudding seems too runny, return to the
oven, checking every 15 minutes, until it is
loosely creamy; the cooking time will vary,
depending on the depth of the baking dish.

5 Remove from the oven and allow to rest for
10 minutes before serving.

Eton Mess

Serves 4 · Preparation and cooking 20 minutes

450g (16oz) strawberries, hulled
and halved

2 tablespoons icing (confectioner's) sugar

250ml (9fl oz/1 cup) cream, 35% fat

4 meringue nests, crumbled

1 Puree half the strawberries with the sugar
   and a little water in a food processor and
   pass through a fine sieve.

2 Lightly whisk the cream until it holds
   soft peaks.

3 Layer the crumbled meringue into serving
   glasses with the whipped cream and
   remaining strawberries. Drizzle over the
   strawberry puree and serve immediately.

Pancakes

Serves 4 · Preparation and cooking 20 minutes

110g (4oz/1 cup) plain (all-purpose) flour

1 teaspoon white (granulated) sugar

1 pinch salt

1 egg

300ml (11fl oz/1⅓ cups) milk

1 teaspoon oil or melted butter

oil for cooking

To serve

white (granulated) sugar

lemon wedges

1. Sift the dry ingredients into a mixing bowl and make a well in the centre. Add the egg and beat well.

2. Add half the milk and the oil and beat until smooth. Stir in the rest of the milk until blended.

3. Lightly oil a pancake or frying pan (skillet) and heat until smoking hot. Add enough batter for a thin, even coating. Cook until set and lightly golden then turn over and cook for another 30 seconds. Remove from the pan and repeat with the remaining batter, greasing the pan between each pancake.

4. Slide the cooked pancakes onto a warm plate, layering up the pancakes with non-stick baking paper, so they don't stick together. Keep warm in a low oven.

5. Fold the pancakes into quarters and serve with sugar for sprinkling and lemon wedges.

Apple and Berry Crumble

Serves 4 · Preparation and cooking 1 hour

400g (14oz) cooking apples, peeled, cored and thickly sliced (peeled weight)

85g (3oz) strawberries, halved if large

85g (3oz) blackberries

110g (4oz/$^1/_2$ cup) white (granulated) sugar for fruit, plus 3 tablespoons for crumble

170g (6oz/1$^1/_2$ cups) plain (all-purpose) flour

85g (3oz/$^1/_3$ cup) butter

20g ($^3/_4$oz/$^1/_4$ cup) rolled oats

1 Heat the oven to 190°C (170°C fan/375°F/ gas 5). Grease a baking dish.

2 Mix together the apples, strawberries, blackberries and sugar and put into the baking dish.

3 Put the flour into a mixing bowl and rub in the butter until the mixture resembles fine breadcrumbs, then stir in the sugar and oats.

4 Sprinkle evenly over the fruit and bake for 30–40 minutes until golden brown and the apples are tender. Serve warm with cream or custard.

Pear Crumble Cake

Makes 1 cake · Preparation and cooking 1 hour

For the cake

170g (6oz/³/₄ cup) butter

170g (6oz/³/₄ cup) caster (berry) sugar

2 eggs, beaten

225g (8oz/2 cups) self-raising flour

few drops vanilla extract

4 pears

For the crumble

110g (4oz/1 cup) self-raising flour

85g (3oz/¹/₃ cup) butter

2 tablespoons caster (berry) sugar

water

To decorate

icing (confectioner's) sugar

For the cake

1 Heat the oven to 160ºC (140ºC fan/320ºF/ gas 3). Grease a deep 18cm (7in) square cake tin and line the base with non-stick baking paper.

2 Beat the butter and sugar in mixing bowl until pale and fluffy. Gradually beat in the eggs.

3 Fold in the flour, then stir in the vanilla. Spread the mixture in the tin.

4 Peel, core and chop the pears and scatter on top of the cake mixture, pressing them down a little.

For the crumble

1 Put the flour into a bowl and rub in the butter until the mixture resembles coarse breadcrumbs. Stir in the sugar and a little water until the mixture sticks together in small crumbs. Sprinkle the crumble evenly over the pears.

2 Bake for 25–35 minutes until the crumble is golden and the cake is cooked through. Cool in the tin and sift over a little icing (confectioner's) sugar when cold. Cut into squares to serve.

Carrot Cake

Makes 1 cake · Preparation and cooking 1 hour 15 minutes

170g (6oz/1½ cups) self-raising flour

2 teaspoons mixed spice

1 pinch salt

150ml (5fl oz/⅔ cup) sunflower oil

170g (6oz/¾ cup) light brown sugar

3 eggs

250g (9oz) carrots, grated

To finish

icing (confectioner's) sugar

1 Heat the oven to 180°C (160°C fan/350°F/ gas 4). Grease a 1kg (2.2lb) loaf tin and line the base with non-stick baking paper.

2 Sift the flour, spice and salt into a mixing bowl. Stir in the remaining ingredients until well mixed.

3 Pour into the tin and bake for 50–60 minutes, until firm to the touch and a skewer inserted into the middle comes out clean. Cool in the tin for 10 minutes, then place on a wire rack to cool completely.

4 Sift over a little icing (confectioner's) sugar.

Lemon Madeleines

Makes 12 · Preparation and cooking 30 minutes + 20 minutes standing

170g (6oz/1½ cups) plain (all-purpose) flour

1 teaspoon baking powder

2 eggs

75g (2½oz/¾ cup) icing (confectioner's) sugar

1 unwaxed lemon, finely grated zest

1 tablespoon lemon juice

85g (3oz/⅓ cup) butter, melted and cooled

1 Heat the oven to 190ºC (170ºC fan/375ºF/gas 5). Butter and flour 12 madeleine moulds.

2 Sift the flour and baking powder into a bowl.

3 Whisk the eggs and icing (confectioner's) sugar in a mixing bowl with an electric whisk until thick and creamy. Gently fold in the lemon zest and juice until blended.

4 Fold in the flour mixture alternately with the melted butter. Leave to stand for 20 minutes.

5 Spoon into the moulds and bake for 8–10 minutes until golden brown. Place on a wire rack to cool completely.

Chocolate Roulade

Makes 1 · Preparation and cooking 50 minutes

For the cake

110g (4oz/1/2 cup) caster (berry) sugar,
plus extra for sprinkling

4 eggs

75g (21/2oz/3/4 cup) plain
(all-purpose) flour

30g (1oz/1/4 cup) cocoa powder,
plus extra for sprinkling

1 tablespoon hot water

For the filling

200ml (7fl oz/7/8 cup) cream, 48% fat

few drops vanilla extract

1–2 tablespoons icing
(confectioner's) sugar

To decorate

whitecurrants

For the cake

1   Heat the oven to 220°C (200°C fan/430°F/
    gas 7). Grease a 23cm x 33cm (9in x 13in)
    Swiss roll tin and line with non-stick
    baking paper.

2   Place the sugar and eggs in a mixing bowl
    and whisk until very pale and light, using an
    electric whisk, until the beaters leave a trail
    on the surface.

3   Sift in the flour and cocoa powder and gently
    fold into the egg mixture using a metal spoon.
    Lightly stir in the hot water until blended.

4   Pour into the prepared tin, tilting it so
    that it covers the whole surface. Bake
    for 7–9 minutes until firm and springy
    to the touch.

5   Sprinkle a sheet of non-stick baking paper
    (a little larger than the tin) with 2 teaspoons
    caster (berry) sugar. Sift 2 tablespoons
    cocoa powder onto the paper.

6   Turn out the cake on to the sugared paper.
    Peel away the lining paper and trim the
    edges. Roll up the cake loosely lengthways,
    with the paper inside and leave to cool
    completely.

For the filling

1   Whisk the cream, vanilla and icing
    (confectioner's) sugar until thick.

2   Unroll the cake and remove the paper.
    Spread the filling over the cake and roll up,
    with the help of the paper. Don't worry if it
    cracks – this is normal.

3   Sift over a little cocoa powder and decorate
    with whitecurrants.

Weights and Measures

Weights and measures differ from country to country, but with these handy conversion charts cooking has never been easier!

Cup Measurements

One cup of these commonly used ingredients is equal to the following weights.

Ingredient	Metric	Imperial
Apples (dried and chopped)	125g	4½oz
Apricots (dried and chopped)	190g	6¾oz
Breadcrumbs (packet)	125g	4½oz
Breadcrumbs (soft)	55g	2oz
Butter	225g	8oz
Cheese (shredded/grated)	115g	4oz
Choc bits	155g	5½oz
Coconut (desiccated/fine)	90g	3oz
Flour (plain/all-purpose, self-raising)	115g	4oz
Fruit (dried)	170g	6oz
Golden (corn) syrup	315g	11oz
Honey	315g	11oz
Margarine	225g	8oz
Nuts (chopped)	115g	4oz
Rice (cooked)	155g	5½oz
Rice (uncooked)	225g	8oz
Sugar (brown)	155g	5½oz
Sugar (caster/berry/superfine)	225g	8oz
Sugar (granulated)	225g	8oz
Sugar (sifted, icing/confectioner's)	155g	5½oz
Treacle (molasses)	315g	11oz

Oven Temperatures

Celsius	Fahrenheit	Gas mark
120	250	1
150	300	2
160	320	3
180	350	4
190	375	5
200	400	6
220	430	7
230	450	8
250	480	9

Liquid Measures

Cup	Metric	Imperial
¼ cup	63ml	2¼fl oz
½ cup	125ml	4½fl oz
¾ cup	188ml	6⅔fl oz
1 cup	250ml	8¾fl oz
1¾ cup	438ml	15½fl oz
2 cups	500ml	17½fl oz
4 cups	1 litre	35fl oz

Spoon	Metric	Imperial
¼ teaspoon	1.25ml	$\frac{1}{25}$fl oz
½ teaspoon	2.5ml	$\frac{1}{12}$fl oz
1 teaspoon	5ml	$\frac{1}{6}$fl oz
1 tablespoon	15ml	½fl oz

Weight Measures

Metric	Imperial
10g	¼oz
15g	½oz
20g	¾oz
30g	1oz
60g	2oz
115g	4oz (¼lb)
125g	4½oz
145g	5oz
170g	6oz
185g	6½oz
200g	7oz
225g	8oz (½lb)
300g	10½oz
330g	11½oz
370g	13oz
400g	14oz
425g	15oz
455g	16oz (1lb)
500g	17½oz (1lb 1½oz)
600g	21oz (1lb 5oz)
650g	23oz (1lb 7oz)
750g	26½oz (1lb 10½oz)
1000g (1kg)	35oz (2lb 3oz)

Index